RESILIENT HEART

By
Shelbie Jo Ann Ledford-Wohlstadter

Foreword by
Bruce Veach

Published by Another 8 Hours Publishing
O'Fallon, Illinois
http://www.Another8Hours.com

ISBN, print ed. 978-0-9828585-5-4

First Printing November 2012

Printed in United States of America

Table of Contents

Acknowledgements

To my father, "The Outlaw," thank you for being who you are, my Dad.

To my wonderful husband, Matt, who has chosen me all along. I love you more and more every day.

To my best friend, Bruce, you're the reason this happened. You're everything good in the world and more. I couldn't and wouldn't ask for a better friend.

To my grandmother, I miss you. I hope you can see all that I am doing and be proud of who I have become. I have never forgotten. You're always on my mind.

To Hayden, Madeline, and Cody, I love you three more than anything.

To all the people who didn't believe in me. Thank you! Without you, I wouldn't be who I am today.

Foreword

On February 21, 1978, I know exactly what I was doing. You might find it strange that nearly 35 years after an event someone would have such a vivid memory, but this was no ordinary occurrence in a 13-year-old boy's life. You see, I was part of a team from a small little school that was about to make history. We were about to defeat big, bad Whiteside in a basketball game. A feat, which my school had rarely achieved prior to that night, and one it certainly hasn't accomplished since.

I bring this up because you think something like that would be the most important thing that would have happened to a 13-year-old boy in Southwestern Illinois on that evening, but it wasn't. As fate would have it, across the country in Woodinville, Washington that very same day the most significant person that didn't adopt me, or come to be because I created them, was being born. A person who I wouldn't even know existed for the next 31 years. A person named Shelbie Ledford.

Shelbie's journey took her from Washington to Arizona and eventually to St Louis. While the specifics of the journey are unimportant, it is important to point out there was no yellow brick road clearly marking her path to happiness and success. Her trail was not clearly marked with flashing detour and warning signs, well, in fairness, they may have been there, but she perhaps didn't see them as she was texting, or singing, or applying make-up.

Nonetheless, it is fair to say she occasionally wandered down the wrong path a time or two on her journey.

I am very happy to report, that of late she has been seeing things more clearly. She has been detouring away from danger and staying more true to the proper path. She has her Emerald City clearly in her sights. However, as she took the journey that brought her to where she is today, we are all very fortunate the she documented her thoughts in writing. We are even more fortunate that she decided to share those thoughts with the world.

I do think about that game against Whiteside quite often because when you're David and you slay Goliath it is something you never forget. However, I know beyond the shadow of a doubt the most important thing that occurred in my life that night was the birth of the best friend I have ever known; she is kind, smart, creative, caring, and beautiful inside and out. I invite you to discover what I have known for a long time, that Shelbie is very talented. Please enjoy her journey.

Bruce Veach, Comedian

The Beginning

Her with her paper dolls;

Strawberry blonde hair.

Her big blue eyes comprehending death for the first time.

A death of a family,

Her brother;

His tears.

She could see the blood from his face so clearly.

Her father,

A wonderful man,

But a man who was never around.

Her Mother,

A dark blank face,

So stale—

Riddled with darkness.

The little girl with her strawberry blonde hair.

Her wooden dolls and matchbox cars.

Found her world to be full of sorrow.

She only knew that behind the trees and half wilted

flowers,

That this would be the world she grew in.

For others, an unexplored world of terror.

Music

I sit.

Reading lyrics

Like the story of my life.

Wondering

If anyone feels this aching

Like I do when I hear the words.

Do you know the meaning?

I ask myself.

The paper burns;

So does my heart.

I feel his voice deep in my mind.

I can't seem to let it go.

I feel what he is feeling.

Music.

Beating through my thoughts;

Wasting away.

Listening to my life on the radio.

Does this man singing know me?

Do I?

I sit.

Reading lyrics.

Like the story of my life.

Music.

America

Standing on the sidelines.

Watching from a distance.

Trying to make sense out of everything.

Wondering...

Are we next?

Praying...

Feeling helpless.

Waiting for the day everything will change

What should I tell the angel that's down the hall?

Maybe I've brought you into a world full of hate.

People can't find peace;

They can't settle their differences.

So because of their selfishness,

We will suffer.

I wish I could protect him,

But I have no idea how I can;

I'm frozen.

Our lives in the hands of a government I know I don't trust.

People are getting sick—

Dying.

The United States of America hanging by a string.

Dangling...

Will we all give up?

Or will America unite in a way God will be touched?

Where our children live in a world
Our grandparents remember.

People will feel safe again.

The American Dream

Will become the world's anchor.

Keeping all safe as one mind

As one—

United.

Father

My Father,

A man of many hats:

A mother;

A father;

A brother;

A son.

You can follow the tracks of his iron boots,

Through the mountain tops out West.

Just don't be alarmed when you find him,

With an angel by his side.

He is an Outlaw they say,

A man of pride a man of honor.

A hero;

A soldier;

An all American Cowboy.

He has danced with death a million times.

Stood for his country when all the rest turned silently away.

He is a sinner;

An artist;

A conservative man;

A saint.

You might find him two-stepping somewhere in the moon
light,

Or working his garden in the early morn.

He has seen sorrow.

He has lived a dream.

An Outlaw they call him;

A man with a dream.

His breath breathes of Whiskey,

Only when his heart bleeds.

A marine

A barrel blazing American man.

You might find him sitting watching the bright sunsets,

Or reminiscing in the moonlight all the places he's been,

An Outlaw they call him.

A man of his word.

He is my Father.

My mentor;

My Hero;

My Dad.

Toxic

It's the whisper I felt on the back of my neck.

The breath of hot air telling me I was a mess.

Reminding me I wasn't good enough to walk in your

shadow.

Always blaming me.

Always telling me how much prettier the other girls were.

Telling me I was lucky.

Rubbing my nose in shit;

Every chance you could get.

The stale whiskey seeping through your pores like sweat.

I spent time making a home for you to punch holes in.

I spent money and enabled you and your habits.

I wear the one thing you ever bought me.

Left arm.

I watched it run out of time and stop.

That's how worthless it I was.

To you a ten dollar watch that can't and refuses to tell time.

I placed my heart in your hands;

Believed the lies;

And even started to believe my own.

Lock me in.

Shut the door.

To cry and pray to God to show me something good.

I would beg and plead and ask why me again.

I was owned by you.

I felt I couldn't breathe.

If I said one thing wrong or had a friend,

Something was wrong.

You would fight me.

Fight, fight, fight, fight, fight....

Until my face was slammed against a door.

Until the blood from my lip,

Fell from my eyes.

Glitter

Glitter,

Like the ocean waves in the moonlight.

How beautiful you are.

The glimmer in your eyes;

Not a care in the world.

Dripping ice cream on a blazing hot day.

Laughing in the shower.

Singing *One More Night* at the top of your lungs.

Patiently waiting for the Tooth Fairy to come,

Only to fall fast asleep.

Waking to find three more dollars than expected,

And being so grateful.

My son is a magical being.

That holds my heart close to his.

Always worried if I am hurt or sad.

He is the sunshine when it rains.

The blessing that is mine.

A Day

I start today

Not worrying about the inevitable.

Placing myself in good things.

Living the day like I am determined to make a difference.

Not molding to someone else's beliefs.

Standing proud.

Standing free.

Starting today with a bold, dramatic heart.

Loving who I am.

Who I have been and who I will be.

Today.

Control

I find it hard to believe you still try to control me.

After all these years,

Always finding some way to hurt me.

Funny thing.

I am stronger than you will ever be.

You stand behind your money and your toys.

I stand in front with an army behind me;

Loving me,

Caring for me.

When all you have is the people you play dolls with.

Playing God;

Controlling their every little move.

You

Remember where you came from.

When you do,

it will settle you back into your shoes,

And humble you.

Don't try too hard to be something you're not.

Be who you are and proud of what you fall for.

Hayden

Standing;

Watching his tears.

So Sad;

I walk away.

Patiently,

I fight the welting tears...

Embarrassed,

Trying to find what will make him smile.

Family

Families are not just the people you were born into.

They are the people that stand next to you when things are tough.

They don't judge you, or manipulate you.

They always believe in you, even when the world shuts you out.

I have learned a lot about family this past year.

I have seen how no matter how far away, mine are always there.

No matter how low I am they stand beside me, waiting for me to take a breath.

They always help me to realize I am better than those who bring me down.

Family is something many don't have.

Some have large families and some small.

Some just have friends to comfort their fall.

My family is made up of so many different types of people.

People that I have crossed paths with in one part of my life—

good or bad.

Some have been there since day one.

Some have been around a month or so.

They all have molded me somehow.

The ones that have stuck are the ones I am glad stood by me.

The ones that have left are just not strong pieces in my puzzle of life.

I have come to know and understand that real family is hard to come by.

I have learned from the secrets of family.

I learned that secrets kill families one day at a time.

My friends and family have seen my soul unwrapped—

raw, and blazing with ugliness.

But they know me.

They know where I stand.

I speak my mind with confidence that they will love me anyway.

They know deep down my soul is pure and beautiful.

I have a few scars here and there.

Nothing too deep or noticeable, I was able to paint over those wounds with knowledge.

Knowledge I hope to share with my children someday.

I will do my best to never take advantage of what I have.

Sometimes life gets too hectic to really soak in and be thankful for what you have.

I will always take a moment for those around me.

And remember that is what life is about.

If I could give all of you a couple words of advice, it would be…

"Love Deeply."

Haunting

A year later,

Still bruised,

Faint black and blue.

Still a hint of beer lingers in the air.

My eyes are wide with wonder.

Still wondering why.

Why I would ever walk down a path of torture.

Knowing from the beginning it was wrong.

I still suffer tremors.

Anxiety riddles me;

Constantly fighting.

Finding new ways to cope.

I stand burning.

Another day;

Smoldering in ashes.

Digging my way out.

Only wishing to be free;

Free of thinking about you;

Free of being reminded.

I will find how to make you stop

Haunting me...

Patiently

I waited for you
Patiently
Fighting thoughts that creep into my mind.
Waiting
Patiently
Tapping
Quietly drifting
Waiting
Pretending
Patiently
Wandering
Counting steps
Waiting
Seems I am unable to control time
Slowly fading into the background
Patiently
Becoming a fixture in your world
Like a lost child in bright yellow clothes
But blending in plain view
Quietly
Dreaming
For you to notice me
Waiting for you
Patiently

Grandmother

Soft…
Her hands;
Her eyes;
Her voice.
Beauty is her.
It was her invention.
Her bright and amazing being.
She was an angel even before death;
A true saint.
Not tainted like all the rest.
When she spoke the world would hear her.
A woman that paid attention,
A woman that listened more than she spoke restless babble.
She is someone I miss around this time,
More I think now than ever.
She used to say I would forget her,
But I believe I love her more now.
Think of her daily.
Miss her greatly.

Black Sun

Black sun;

Wakened to a world of chaos.

Anarchy;

Faith fading like mist.

Communism;

Spreading like fire.

Their theories distorted.

Their non-intellectual minds building a world of hate.

For years our country has saved others.

Hated more now than ever.

Results war,

And our flagged burned.

Freedom...

Never...

Just the blood that drips from our heroes.

Believe in Me

Written By Jamie Jones & Shelbie Wohlstadter

Sometimes it seems
Things just don't seem the way they are
When you're laying by my side.

I guess you would say
Dreams are the things that never die
Even when you're falling apart.

Believe in me
And all your dreams
Will somehow come true.

Hold onto love and we will make it through,
With everything we do.

Slowly, your love
Just fades away
From my heart.
But as hard as I try
I can't help but wonder why
"I still love you".

Believe in me
And all your dreams
Will somehow come true.

Believe in me
And while you dream
Remember that I am here
And always will be.

Hold onto love
It'll guide you through
With everything you do.

-Believe in me

Fake

Why can't I just pretend?

Pretend that my life is perfection.

No one sees my hurt.

And for some reason, I am numb to their ignorance.

Let them believe the lies in their head.

Let them believe my tears never ran red.

Let them think my scars aren't real.

Vast attempts of suicide.

They will never understand.

No one can.

I don't.

I am so fake;

So unreal.

And yet not a person in the world, including me,

Doesn't care.

Grandpa

Have I seen you before?

Beautiful face,

Like an angel.

Have you come to save us?

Are you just passing through?

Why does it feel like I know you?

I know those eyes,

That unbelievable smile.

I knew you a long time ago,

Do you remember?

I saw you.

You knew me,

You guided me;

Taught me about respect.

Don't you remember me?

Grandpa....

Broken

Light

Blinding

Open your eyes

See what lies before you

Absolutely nothing

Just a memory

To him

The memories mean nothing

To him a waste of time

You Love

You Lose

He wins.

Or so you think

Your soul taken and shattered

All that is left are your tears

His life just starting

Yours ending

Darkness

That's all you see

Dreams of him

Loving him

Wondering

Does he ever think of you?

Finding him pretending
Why?
You're confused
He is so calm
His life all figured out
A life you're not even apart of anymore

Dark Faces

Every day I struggle between two separate worlds.

Worlds I feel I know nothing about.

I have a new family,

And a 10-year-old boy.

His anger;

Starting to surface,

Slowly.

A cry for help.

A cry...

For me to listen.

If I explained,

Would he understand?

Should I blanket him in lies?

He will still blame me.

Every day I come home to eyes that seem very strange to me.

Eyes of a child,

I use to know and understand.

Now,

He seems so far away.

I reminisce about the times he looked to me.

His big blue eyes depended on me.

The way he always wanted me there,

Every second of everyday.

Now, he could care less if I walk in the door at night.

I feel I have lost him.

I have lost his love.

His Trust...I have lost him.

Never

Living in my dreams.

Day after day,

Not really facing reality.

In my mind, that's okay.

Losing my thoughts;

My feelings;

My values come and go.

I feel so many different ways.

People come,

But they will always leave someday.

I never know where and when I am going.

I never know what to say.

I've always felt a little out of touch with people.

But in my mind, that's okay.

Sounds of Music

It's funny to think how music can bring you to a place you
have been before.

In an instant,

Music brings back memories you've tucked secretly away.

Never to open again.

But music can,

Like a stepping stool of memories.

Some good;

Some bad.

Either way you will always remember.

A time;

A tear;

A laugh.

In any breath of your life.

Gossip

Confident…

Walk Confident.

You're better than them.

The whispering woman in the hall,

They hate that you smile and laugh all the time.

They want to talk smack and have it float into your ears

to make you frown on yourself.

Don't let them get to you.

Love who you are.

You dream bigger and brighter than they would ever be

able to.

It's hard for their little minds to comprehend

That beauty is only beauty if you possess the right tools.

Otherwise it's skin deep.

So let them talk and banter on,

Because no matter what,

You are who you are and you're worth happiness.

Little Moments

Sitting,

Watching him sleep.

Wondering what he's dreaming.

His little hands,

His little feet.

So innocent,

So sweet.

Room

Lamp lighted room...

Focus on the pure mystery of time...

Focus on every soul that has passed through.

All the people you use to know...

They will all remember you this way.

In this room,

It was the first time you laughed.

It was the first time you said.

It was the first time he saw you.

In this room.

Where are they all now?

The mystery of life...

All told by this very room.

All the things you seem to forget...

The Room Remembers

Hold

Step back...

Take a look at your life.

Blinding...

Cherish it.

Remember this very moment...

The moment you stepped forward.

It's now time to focus on the future.

Shut the door to what use to be,

Open the door to what could be.

Once in awhile you forget to breathe in.

Don't let the small things bother you.

You're a soldier...

Embrace it.

It's funny how fast things pass you by.

Sometimes there isn't enough time to hold on.

Just a glimpse...

Of something that might have been.

Pay attention,

It might pass you by.

Flowers...

Lean over...

Smell the flowers.

Dream...

Hold on to them...

Try to fulfill them the best you can.

Giving up now?

No,

You've only just begun.

Chin up...

Smile.

Emptiness

Look,

Within her eyes.

So dark;

So empty.

Although it looks as if

She has it all,

Her tears fall.

Slowly dripping onto the floor.

Beautiful;

Sweet.

But nothing

Nothing to live for...

Slipping

Don't let me fade

Hold on

As tight as you can

Can you feel me slipping further

There isn't anything I can do

Just let me go

I've already given up

I can't be here anymore

I can't breathe the air here

It suffocates me

I am broken

Slipping

Small Flickering Flames

Your mouth moves

Little white lies

Small flickering flames

Your one lie away from burning my whole world

Sending it all up into flames

Lie

Lie to me

You believe your own lies

You've fabricated in your sick brain

Small flickering flames

Drowning my lungs in pain

Lie

Crazy liar

Sociopathic

It's who you are

Small flickering flames

You'll never love anyone

Only your selfish need to deceive.

Your mouth moves

Little white lies

Small flickering flames
Your one lie away from burning my world
Sending it all up into flames

Trusting you
Was a mistake for me
It was a mind altering
Everyday
Too much time wasted
Sort of thing.

Your mouth moves
Little white lies
Small flickering flames
Your one lie away from burning my whole world
Sending it up into flames

I don't need apologies
I need the truth
About who you are
Who you would like to be
Don't cry to me
I have spent too much time
Spilling tears over you
It's time now to let you go

Let you burn alone
Your mouth moves
Little white lies
Small flickering flames
Your one lie away from burning my whole world
Sending it up into flames

Beautiful

She is beautiful;
Pale faced;
Bright blue eyes.
A woman of grace,
A woman of respect.

She is torn in so many ways.
Always wanting what should've been;
What could've been.
Never appreciative of what stands before her.

She is selfish;
Bitter…
A brilliant soul.
A brilliant soul full of despair.
She falls asleep at night with tears in her eyes.
A pretender to everyone around her.
No one know the hurt she endures.

She is beautiful;
Pale faced;
Bright blue eyes.
Pride full…
Blessed.

One card short of a full house,
She stays in the game.
Knowing she will lose.

All she wants is him to hold her all night long.
She wants him to love her,
The same way she loves him.
Someday she says,
Someday even in death it will happen.

She is beautiful;
Pale faced;
Bright blue eyes are hopeful,
Determined…
Yet broken.

Time

We all need a little more time...

Do you ever wonder where it goes?

One minute you are learning to ride a bike;

The next a car.

And sooner than later,

You can't do anything on your own.

Sooner than later, you slowly vanish.

Everything you were...

Just a memory to those who knew you.

Another Day

Rises and falls
Tired little feet
Ready for the weekend
What I wouldn't do to be free for one day
To walk somewhere
Anywhere
Waste my daydreaming
Dreaming about a life I will never have
Maybe eat ice cream and watch children play
Pretend I am them
Swing
Round and round on the carousel
Skipping
To be a child again
To be free
Another day passes
Fast
Sometimes too fast to speak of
We end up 50 before we know it
Tired
Tired of running my thoughts
One day… Maybe
I'll be free

Best Friend

Many would falter,
But with you I know you would throw me a hand.
I can be enlightened,
Without true understanding.
But you always try to get me;
Analyze my thoughts.
You place my dreams in front of yours,
Even when your talents sore above mine.
I can fall one day,
But you find a way to boast me up.
A laugh;
A heart to heart;
Or just an ear to listen.
A completely selfless person,
When I am selfish to the core.
An even match I'd say,
Maybe just the perfect balance.
A brother;
An ally;
The best friend ever.
What you are to me…
There isn't a word or a phrase to sum it up completely.
But I know in short,
I adore you…
My Best Friend.

About the Author

Shelbie Jo Ann Ledford-Wohlstadter is no stranger to abuse, heartache, and pain—physical and emotional. Born to a schizophrenic mother in Woodinville, Washington the abuse started just months into her life. She was separated from her sibling brother, left to fend for herself as she was constantly removed from her home by her mother while the effects of the illness drove her to do the unthinkable.

At the age of six Shelbie had lived through more than most people live in a lifetime. It was then her father finally divorced her mother, moved to Arizona, and she was rejoined with her brother. Under the care and guidance of her father and paternal grandmother she finally started to see a life of normalcy. That was, until her brother went off to the military and she entered a world of depression.

During the high school years her world was once again flipped upside down. She began experimenting and making wrong choices in her actions as well as the people she befriended. When she ended up pregnant her junior year the family she had come to rely on shut the door on her, leaving her homeless. She ended up married to the father of her son, only to have it end in divorce after years of neglect, fighting, and infidelities.

Desiring an escape from it all Shelbie headed to the St. Louis area where she made a fresh start with the help of a friend. Later she would fall in love, remarry, and have another son. Within a few years the depression hit again after the passing of her grandmother and her eldest son going to live with his father. As a result, her marriage was thrown into turmoil as she turned to another man—a man who would take her back to the familiar world of mental and physical abuse. No longer able to handle it all, Shelbie slowly slipped into a life of self-destruction that would ultimately lead to a mental breakdown and a stint in rehab.

By the grace of God, her husband stuck by her through the worst of times. She made the decision to rid her life of the toxic people to make room for those who would build her up and support her. Everything has now come together. She sees brightness in her future and is once again a confident woman.

Writing was the only thing that kept Shelbie sane. It helped her to escape a lot of emotions that could've eaten her alive if left alone. Placing them on paper allowed her to release them from her soul.

CPSIA information can be obtained
at www.ICGtesting.com
Printed in the USA
FFOW01n0631060217
32088FF